QUICK & EASY PARTY TREATS

FOR SPECIAL OCCASIONS

I. NGEOW

CONTENTS

INTRODUCTION

Everybody has special occasions with friends and family at home. I believe the celebration is in the company, and in saving us time and money on catering. My ideal party is a nice dress and earrings, quick bites and sparkling drinks and conversation, dinner, refreshments, coffee and dessert, crowding around the piano for a live impromptu 1980s singalong soiree, with two or three guests looking up lyrics on their phones, accompanied by yours truly. That is my idea of a relaxing and enjoyable time.

I am a regular, busy, family person just like you. Who isn't? I am not a chef or a caterer. I haven't got all day and I will not be waking up at 5am to cook (to write, yes, but that's a different story).

If you are overwhelmed by the concept of catering for your own parties, it's time to celebrate. These 5 modern appetizers and a bonus cocktail are quick and easy to make. They can be made in batches and in a small kitchen with little effort yet making a big impression. Most importantly, they are healthy, low-salt and low-fat compared to shop-bought alternatives. Many steps can also be prepared in advance so you will have more time to relax and enjoy yourself at your party. Perfect for those who would like to do entertain guests but don't know how to or where to start. Included is my original vintage-inspired Asian cocktail, *Halong Bay*.

Make special occasions extra special with homemade treats. If you like delicious and healthy fun-to-make snacks, you'll love *Quick and Easy Party Treats*.

Bon appetit. Bonsoir.

Thank you for reading.

- Perfect for beginners at entertaining
- Light and easy modern cuisine
- Quick preparation anyone can do
- Minimal or no cooking
- 5 appetizers and 1 cocktail recipe included
- Great ideas for holidays, birthdays or festive celebrations.

AVOCADO BRUSCHETTA 3-IN-1
MEAL DEAL

Y ou cannot prepare this 3-in-1 much in advance, so use task-batching and create a factory line assembly. In actual fact it will take minutes, as basically, it's toast.

Serves 6

- Olive oil
- One loaf whole grain baguette
- 6 radishes thinly sliced
- 6 cups of rocket or watercress
- 2 cucumbers shaved thinly into ribbons using vegetable peeler
- 2 avocados, smashed
- 1 tbsp fresh lime juice
- Sea salt to taste
- Ground black pepper
- 4 large tomatoes, chopped
- 1 clove garlic cut into half
- 1 clove garlic finely minced
- 2 tbsp olive oil
- 1 tbsp balsamic vinegar
- 3-4 basil leaves, finely chopped

Instructions

1. Preheat grill to high. Cut baguette into ½" thick oval slices. Count the number of slices and roughly divide by 3. Keep this number in mind, eg X.
2. Place the ovals on baking sheet, brush with oil and sprinkle with sea salt. Toast for 2-3 minutes or until light golden and a bit crispy-looking.
3. Remove from grill and rub the top side with the cut halves of the garlic clove.
4. In a medium bowl, smash the avocado and mix in lime juice, sea salt to taste.

5. In another bowl, combine the chopped tomato, olive oil and balsamic vinegar.
6. In a separate large bowl, put in the chopped tomatoes, olive oil, minced garlic and balsamic vinegar. Mix gently but not too much as it will start to crush the tomatoes.
7. Spread the avocado mixture onto all the slices of toast.
8. Put 1 tbsp tomato onto X number of slices.
9. Put 1 tbsp sliced radish onto the second X number of slices.
10. Put 1 cucumber ribbon on each slice of the remaining third. Top with a few rocket or watercress leaves.
11. Grind fresh black pepper on all the slices of toast. Garnish with chopped basil on the tomatoey ones.

SMOKED SALMON & CREAM CHEESE TOWERS

F or those who enjoy a bit of construction, here's vertical food you can be proud of. Looks so impressive and artistic and yet so easy. Trust me, I'm an architect.

Serves 6

- 2 packets of smoked salmon
- 2 tubs of cream cheese
- 1 jar of black caviar
- 1 cucumber
- Dash of black pepper
- Juice of 2 lemons or lemons cut into thin wedges and left ready to use
- Dill and cherry tomatoes (halved) to garnish

1. Cut the cucumber into thin circular slices first and then halve those so that from each slice you will get 2 semi-circle blades.
2. Take each slice of smoked salmon and cut it into half lengthways, so that it becomes two strips. Using a flat spatula, roughly place 1 tbsp of cream cheese on one end of the strip. Sprinkle some fresh black ground pepper over the strip.
3. Roll the salmon strip tightly from the end with the blob first and make the tower stand up. Tuck the flap of salmon strip end in the bottom of the tower like when you tuck a sheet in for making the bed. The tower should be 1" in diameter, and 2" maximum height. If it is less than an inch in diameter and higher than 2" it will not stand up.
4. Stab in the cucumber semi-circle blade into the top of the "turban", making sure that around ½" sticks out at the top. Put ½ tsp of black caviar on top of the "turban". Garnish with a sprig of dill. Decorate serving dish with cherry tomatoes. Drizzle over with lemon juice or leave wedges ready for guests to do the squeezing themselves.

ROAST DUCK AND LEEK WONTONS

This is a Chinese-inspired recipe which is fun and very professional-looking. **HOT TIP #1:** substitute the roast duck for grilled tofu to make this dish vegan. **HOT TIP #2:** You can pre-make the wonton cups up to a week in advance and store in an airtight container to keep fresh.

Serves 6 (makes 24)

- Spray oil
- 24 wonton wrappers or skins
- Hoisin sauce in squeeze bottle
- 2 tsp sesame oil
- 2 tbsp lime juice
- 1 tsp grated fresh ginger
- ½ cucumber, cut lengthways, stripped into ribbons using a vegetable peeler
- ½ leek, thinly sliced
- ½ Chinese barbecue duck or Peking-style ready roasted duck breast stripped into shreds and finely chopped OR firm tofu cut into ½" cubes
- 2 green spring onions, thinly sliced
- 2 tsp toasted sesame seeds (1 tsp black and 1 tsp white)
- Herbs, finely minced, to garnish eg parsley or coriander (cilantro)
- Dip: Chilli garlic sauce or Sriracha chilli sauce to serve (optional)

Method

1. Preheat oven to 375°F or 180°C. Preheat grill to maximum. Spray oil onto a 24-hole mini muffin tin.
2. Spray a baking sheet with oil and place the leek slices. If doing vegan option and using tofu instead of duck, place the tofu on the same sheet. Give everybody a good spray. Grill for 2-3 minutes or until both leek and tofu look slightly golden and crisp. Remove from grill and allow to cool.
3. Use an 8cm or 3" cutter to cut out 24 rounds from wonton wrappers. Push a wrapper into each hole, pressing folds against side to form cups. Spray oil onto the wrappers.
4. Bake the wonton cups for 8 minutes or until golden and crisp. Remove from oven and allow to cool.

5. Combine sesame oil, lime juice, ginger, duck meat (OR tofu) and onions in a medium bowl.
6. Fill wonton cups to half with mixture, half with one cross-sectional slice of leek. Roll up one cucumber ribbon and stab it into the cup.
7. Squeeze a small blob of hoisin onto the assembly. Decorate with a sprinkle of black and white sesame seeds and finally top it off with a spring of herb to garnish.
8. Serve with the optional chilli sauce or Sriracha in a separate dip dish.

CHICKEN, CRANBERRY AND BRIE TARTLETS

I 've always loved the red and white combination of brie and cranberry. **HOT TIP #1:** You can prepare up to and including step 5 in advance and store in the fridge if a day or two in advance or on the counter if it's for a few hours. **HOT TIP #2:** If storing in the fridge, use an airtight container, and make sure you let the tartlets warm up to room temperature or put it in the oven again for 2 minutes. Preparing most of the steps in advance will save time until it's ready to be served, because the last step takes a few seconds only— sprinkling herbs.

Serves 6 (makes 24)

- 1½-2 sheets puff pastry
- 1 cooked chicken breast, diced
- ¼ cup brie cut into 24 even pieces
- Small jar of cranberry sauce
- 1 tablespoon finely chopped fresh herbs eg parsley

1. Preheat the oven to 390°F or 220°C conventional or 200°C fan-assisted.
2. Roll and flatten the puff pastry sheet a bit more to make it thinner. Cut into 2½" squares.
3. Line a 24-hole mini muffin baking tray with the squares, letting the edges oversail the muffin tin. Place in the freezer for 15 minutes to firm.
4. Bake "blind" for 10 minutes or golden and crisp. Using a teaspoon, wooden dowel about 1" in diameter, or the back end of a mini hammer, press down the centers to flatten the pastry. Fill with 2 tsp of chicken. Top with a piece of brie and a tsp of cranberry sauce.
5. Re-insert tray into oven and bake for 5-7 minutes or until golden brown to melt the cheese.
6. Sprinkle with chopped herbs.

TOFU GREEN SALAD WITH
CRANBERRY AND MISO DRESSING

A clean lean green salad will balance the richness of finger food, featuring an original east-west fusion Ivy dressing with cranberry and miso that will set off the greens perfectly. **HOT TIP:** to cheat you can also use a mayonnaise containing Dijon mustard to save one ingredient.

Serves 6

- 9 cups of green salad with watercress, rocket and spinach for example
- 2 cups of tofu, lightly grilled on both sides and cut into 1" cubes
- 2 cups of quartered cherry tomatoes
- 3 stalks of spring onions (scallions) thinly chopped

For the dressing

- 1 tsp miso paste
- ½ cup walnut oil
- A dash of sesame oil
- 1 tbsp mayonnaise
- 1 tsp Dijon mustard
- ½ tbsp cranberry sauce
- A splash of Mirin soy sauce
- 1 clove garlic, crushed
- Juice of a lime

1. Put all the salad vegetables in a large wide bowl. Sprinkle the tofu cubes over the top.
2. Put all the dressing ingredients into a large shaker (I use my protein smoothie shaker, lol) or watertight jar and shake hard. Pour over the salad.

BONUS: HALONG BAY COCKTAIL

This is a 1960s vintage-themed original Ivy cocktail and a twist on the classic Red Lotus. Vroom!

Serves 6

- Juice of ½ a lime

- 3 cups of cranberry juice
- 6 jiggers lychee liqueur
- 6 jiggers vodka
- 1 cup lychee juice (from the can)
- 3 cups or more crushed ice
- 6 slices of lime for garnish
- 12 lychees from a can

1 jigger = 1 fl oz

1. Put all the ingredients into in a blender except the last three. Blitz completely.
2. Fill chilled high ball tumblers with 2 lychees each and half fill with crushed ice.
3. Pour cocktail in. Garnish with slices of lime. You may now add a Vietnamese painted paper mini-umbrella to each glass… if you want. Bonsoir, Vietnam!

LIST OF RECIPES

The idea came about for writing this book when I wanted to do an intimate party at home just for family this year. Of course you can always buy party food under the "party food" section of supermarkets but when you study the contents, they are all high in fat, sugar and sodium. Another tip I can give you is that the recipes in this book are suitable for lunch too. Accompanied with noodles or a salad, there is nothing to stop us from amping up and making a proper meal combo. Every weekend can be a bit special.

1. Avocado Bruschetta 3-in-1 meal deal
2. Smoked Salmon and Cream Cheese Towers
3. Roast Duck and Leek Wontons
4. Chicken, cranberry and brie tartlets
5. Tofu Green Salad with Cranberry and Miso Dressing
6. Halong Bay cocktail

JUST IN CASE ONLY

In addition to the 6 items above, if you get a sudden sinking feeling in your heart that there is not enough food or the fear that your mini party will turn major (but you may know this already), standard 6 SOS party measures include:

1. Big bowl of chips or Doritos
2. Small bowl of nuts, surrounded by berries or fruits
3. Big bowl of vegetarian noodles
4. 3 baguettes sliced up and put in a basket
5. 3 different dips (taramasalata, guacamole, houmous)
6. Margherita pizza[1]

I hope you have a smashing time at your party whatever you plan to do.

LOVE CHINESE FOOD BUT DON'T HAVE TIME?

Ivy's practical solution is an easy cookbook for families and the time-poor to start making delicious and healthy Chinese food at home. Read *30 Chinese Dinners: Healthy Easy Homemade Meals.*

---

1. Standby only. To be kept in fridge or freezer until you notice that everything is really, really running out. If you put it in the oven too soon, it will just get cold when it comes out or worse still, you will forget that it's in the oven.

BEFORE YOU GO

The book you are holding in your hand is the result of my dream to be an author. I hope you enjoyed it as much as I enjoyed writing it. I am slowly building my author brand, ranking and profile. As you probably suspected, it takes weeks, months or years to write a book. It exists through dedication, passion and love. Reviews help persuade others to give my books a shot. More readers will motivate me to write, which means more books. I love connecting with and hearing from you. I personally read each review you write. It gives me a sense of fulfilment and meaning— you read my book, I read your review. It will take *less than a minute* and can be only a line to say what you liked or didn't. If you could do me just this one favour and help me, I would be ever so grateful. Please leave me a review anywhere you bought this book. A big thank you. *Ivy*

ABOUT THE AUTHOR

I. Ngeow was born and raised in Johor Bahru, Malaysia. A graduate of the Middlesex University Writing MA programme, Ivy won the 2005 Middlesex University Literary Press Prize out of almost 1500 entrants worldwide. Her debut *Cry of the Flying Rhino* (2017) won the 2016 International Proverse Prize.

Ivy is a regular suburban London mum who likes books, wine and cake. She is an architect and musician with a passion for creative writing since she was a child, winning her first competition at 16. An author of literary suspense thriller novels and short stories, she started writing practical non-fiction lifestyle books to help families or regular, busy and tired people, like herself, to save time and money by cooking and keeping fit at home in modern, quick and easy ways. Her interests include impromptu virtuoso piano performances, health and fitness, beauty and sewing. You can find her here:

writengeow (www.writengeow.com)
Twitter (twitter.com/ivyngeow)
Facebook (facebook.com/ivyngeowwriter)
Instagram (www.instagram.com/ivyngeow)
Email: ivy_ngeow AT yahoo DOT com

ALSO BY I. NGEOW

COOKBOOKS

30 Chinese Dinners: Healthy Easy Homemade Meals

FITNESS

Fitness and Meal Plan Journal: 12-week daily workout and food planner notebook

Amazing at 50: 10-day Flat Tummy Challenge

Awesome at 50: Body Reboot in 6 weeks

DESIGN

Midcentury Modern: 15 Interior Design Ideas

PHOTO CREDITS

Photography by author and the following:

Printed in Great Britain
by Amazon